Country Music Trivia

Frances C. Smith

Raymond E. Smith

Dedicated to

R. L. & Carolyn Hamrick

Introduction

Country musicians first performed on radio in 1922. The following year, station WBAP in Fort Worth, Texas, debuted what's believed to have been the first country music radio "barn dance" - an ensemble variety show that had the feel of a family gathering and was aimed at rural audiences. Eager to exploit radio's advertising power, stations in Chicago (WLS), Nashville (WSM), and elsewhere soon followed suit. The early radio barn dances provided a living for country entertainers throughout the nation while becoming a vital part of listeners' lives. As a distant fan of WLW-Cincinnati's Monday Night in Renfro Valley put it, "You make . . . your folks of Renfro Valley so real to us that we may be coming to Kentucky just to get back to happiness and contentment."

Many country performers bridled at the word "hillbilly," considering it loaded with negative cultural stereotypes. By contrast, "cowboy" implied romance, bravery, and the self-sufficiency of life on the open range. By the mid-1930s, Western fringe and cowboy hats had become part of many singers' wardrobes - including pop stars' - especially after Gene Autry and other Hollywood singing cowboys began to tackle the world's ills in their fantasy version of the West. As Autry wrote of one of his typical movies, "While my solutions were a little less complex than those offered by FDR . . . I played a kind of New Deal cowboy who never hesitated to tackle many of the same problems."

Country Music Trivia

1. What was the name of Alan Jackson's first band?

Dixie Steel

2. When was Ronnie Milsap's 'Daydreams of night things' published?

1975

3. What year did Elvis win best performer?

1981

Country Music Trivia

4. What was Barbara Mandrell's first single?

Queen for a Day

5. Who recorded 'Nobody Falls Like a Fool'?

Earl Thomas Conley

6. What year did Lee Greenwood win 'Male Vocalist of the Year'?

1984

7. Where was Earl Thomas Conley born?

Ohio

8. What was the name of Lee Greenwood's first band?

The Moonbeams

Country Music Trivia

9. Who sang 'One on the Way'?

Loretta Lynn

10. Who sand Southern California with George Jones?

Loretta Lynn

11. Who was CMA's first woman entertainer?

Loretta Lynn

12. What instrument did Tammy Wynette play in the high school band?

Flute

13. What did Larry Gatlin name his autobiography?

All the gold in California

14. What year was 'Behind Closed Doors' released?

1973

15. What song did Emmy Lou Harris release after being made popular by Hank Snow?

I'm Moving On

16. What was some of Garth Brooks early ambitions?

Football and Forest Ranger

17. What group made popular 'Heaven's Just a Sin Away'?

The Kendall's

18. Who made popular 'Talking in Your Sleep'?

Crystal Gayle

19. Which of the Statler Brothers are real brothers?

Country Music Trivia

Harold & Don

29. Where was Crystal Gayle born?

Paintsville, KY

21. Where was Lee Greenwood born?

California

22. In 1996 Lee Greenwood opened his own theater, where?

The Smokey Mts.

23. Who helped Cal Smith get his first music deal?

Ernest Tubb

24. What year was Loretta Lynn elected to the Grand Ole Opry?

1986

25. How old was Hank Williams Jr. when he started singing with his father on stage?

Eight

26. What year was Loretta Lynn elected to the Hall of Fame?

1988

27. How many million albums did George Jones sell?

57

28. Who made 'Bobby Sue' popular in 1982?

The Oak Ridge Boys

Country Music Trivia

29. What business was Donna Fargo's family in?
Tobacco farming

30. Dan Seals' father was a lifetime friend with which singer?
Ernest Tubb

31. Which country female singer got her pilot's license in 1986?
Barbara Mandrell

32. T. G. Sheppard was the nephew of which comedian of the Grand Ole Opry?
Rod Brasfield

33. Who released 'Blanket on the Ground' in 1975?

Billie Jo Spears

34. Where did Dolly Parton grow up?
Locust Ridge, TN

35. George Strait sold the second largest number of Platinum albums, who was number one?
Elvis Presley

36. Who did Dolly Parton sing with on Television for many years?
Porter Waggoner

37. Crystal Gayle was the youngest of how many children?
Eight

Country Music Trivia

38. Billy Crash Craddock was one of how many children?

13

39. What was Gene Watson's occupation before becoming a singer?

Auto body repairman

40. Tammy Wynette retained her former occupation license, what was it?

Beautician

41. What was the theme of Jimmy Roger's songs?

Trains

42. Marty Robbin's enjoyed a sport that took a lot

of his spare time, what was it?

Auto racing

43. Johnny Lee married an actress from the TV show Dallas, who was she?

Charlene Tilton

44. Who was known as the stuttering singer?

Mel Tillis

45. Who made popular the song "Lucille?"

Kenny Rogers

46. What was Eddie Rabbit doing when he was introduced to country music?

On a Boy Scout trip

47. What disease did Eddie Rabbit die of in 1982?

Lung Cancer

48. What did Johnny Cash build with 'One Piece at a Time'?

A Cadillac

49. What was Joe Diffie's occupation before becoming a singer?

Farming

50. Who was known as the man in black?

Johnny Cash

51. Who was Conway Twitty's singing partner for many years?

Country Music Trivia

Loretta Lynn

52. When was the peak of country music?
The '70s

53. Who was the popular mother and daughter duo?
The Judds

54. Who was the coal miner's daughter?
Loretta Lynn

55. What female singer held the title of steer roping?
Reba McEntire

56. What group sold over 65 million albums?
Alabama

57. Who teamed with Willie Nelson to sing 'Seven Spanish Angels'?

Ray Charles

58. Who said, 'All I do is play music and golf'?

Willie Nelson

59. Who made popular 'The Most beautiful Girl in the World'?

Charlie Rich

60. What was Crystal Gale's first name before changing it?

Brenda

61. What TV series did John Conlee appear on?

Hee Haw

62. What was the color of John Conlee's glasses?

Rose colored

63. Bobby Bare sang about the streets of what city?

Baltimore

64. What singer moved to Nashville in 1964 with a guitar and $40.00?

Tom T. Hall

63. What city was Pam Tillis born?

Plant City, FL

66. What patriotic song did lee Greenwood make popular?

Country Music Trivia

God Bless the USA

67. In Dottie West's song what did she say she was raised on"

Country sunshine

68. What popular governor did Linda Ronstadt date?

Jerry Brown

69. What singer was known to carry an open bottle of whiskey on stage?

Merle Haggard

70. What was Moe Bandy's occupation before becoming a singer?

Sheet metal worker

71. What was the male singer of the Kendall's first name?

Royce

72. A stretch of highway I-85 was name after which singer?

Alan Jackson

73. What was Alan Jackson's job before becoming a singer?

Fork lift operator

74. Who originally made the hit "Pop a Top?"

Jim Ed Brown

75. What was country music originally called?

Hillbilly music

Country Music Trivia

76. What was Conway Twitty's real name?

Harold Jenkins

77. What singer was married to Julia Roberts?

Lyle Lovette

78. Who was the first country singer to appear on Saturday Night Live?

Anne Murray

79. Which former Beatles had a hit song with Buck Owens?

Ringo Starr

80. Who were the first singers inducted into the Country Music Hall of Fame?

Hank Williams and Jimmy Rogers

Country Music Trivia

81. What four singers made up the group Highwaymen?

Johnny Cash, Willie Nelson, Waylon Jennings and Kris Kristofferson

82. Who played the part of Loretta Lynn in the film The Coal Miner's Daughter?

Sissy Spacek

83. Which singer was born in Butcher Holler?

Loretta Lynn

84. Which singer was inducted into the Country Music Hall of Fame twice?

Roy Rogers. First with the Sons of the Pioneers and then as an individual

85. Who was the singer and helicopter pilot that

married Rita Coolidge?

Kris Kristofferson

86. Who helped David Frizzell decorate their home?

A wino (In his song)

87. What are the first names of the duo Brooks & Dunn?

Kix and Ronnie

88. Who first recorded 'Friends in Low Places'?

Mark Chesnutt

89. What was Dolly Parton's first top 40 hit?

Dumb Blonde

Country Music Trivia

90. What is said to be the perfect country song?

You Never call me By My Name

91. What song features the line 'The World Must be Flat When People Leave They never Come Back'?

Small Town Saturday Night by Hal Ketchum

92. What singer was shot four times during an attempted robbery in Nashville in 1991?

Tracy Lawrence

93. Who was known as the 'King of Country Swing'?

Bob Wills

94. What song was Reba McEntire singing when she was discovered?

The national Anthem

Country Music Trivia

95. What singer had the most top 40 hits?

George Jones

96. Which singer had the hit 'Whose Bed Have Your Boots Been Under'?

Shania Twain

97. Who recorded 'Tonight the Heartaches on Me'?

The Dixie Chicks

98. What was the Ryman Auditorium first called?

Union Gospel Tabernacle

99. Who wrote the line 'Why Do I let Myself Worry' and in what song?

Willie Nelson in Crazy

Country Music Trivia

100. What group sang Mr. Bojangles?

The Nitty Gritty Dirt Band

101. What singer left the 'First Edition' to sing on his own?

Kenny Rogers

103. What singer is famous for 'Ring of Fire'?

Johnny Cash

104. Which country music star played a football coach in `The Waterboy`?

Jerry Reed

105. What is the name of the charity that Garth Brooks, the country music superstar, has raised in excess of four million dollars?

Ronald McDonald Children's Charities

106. What future country rock star recorded the 1958 pop classic, `It's Only Make Believe`?

Conway Twitty

107. Who was the country music female super star who recorded the 1950's hit `Walking After Midnight`?

Patsy Cline

108. What country music star had a bestselling album called `Sing Me Back Home`?

Merle Haggard

109. Where did country music star Garth Brooks go to college?

Oklahoma State University

110. What country music singer has a theme park?

Country Music Trivia

Dolly Parton

111. What country music legend was known as the `Mississippi Blue Yodeler`?

Jimmy Rogers

112. Who recorded the 1970's country music smash `Satin Sheets'?

Jeannie Pruitt

113. Who was the first living person to become a member of the Country Music Hall of Fame?

Roy Acuff

114. What female country music star died in a plane crash in 1963?

Patsy Cline

115. What city had the most country music talents during the 1920s?

Atlanta, GA

116. Who was known as the Father of Country Music?

Jimmy Rogers

117. Which auto maker put the most money into country music during the 1920s?

Henry Ford

118. Hank Williams did not write most of his songs as he has been given credit. Who was the writer?

Fred Rose

119. Where was Ronnie Milsap born?

Robbinsville, NC

Country Music Trivia

120. Who was Lynn Anderson's mother?

Liz Anderson

121. Where was Willie nelson Born?

In a box car in Oildale, CA

122. What singer charged $2.00 a ticket for people to attend his wedding?

Hank Williams

123. Johnny Duncan was a cousin to what other singer?

Dan Seals

124. What did George Strait do before becoming a singer?

He ran a thousand acre farm in TX

Country Music Trivia

125. What was Don William's nickname?

The Gentle Giant

126. Who made popular 'Don't Rock the Juke Box'?

Alan Jackson

127. When Tammy Wynette and George Jones sang 'Golden Ring' where did the ring re-appear at the end of the song?

A Pawn Shop in Chicago

128. What was Mickey Gilley's first hit song?

Room Full of Roses

129. What group did Ray walker sing with?

The Jordanaires

130. Which of the Statlers are not real brothers?

Phil and Jimmy

131. In the 1975 hit by Conway Twitty who did he say was on his mind?

Linda

132. What popular singer quit singing and became a motivational speaker?

Naomi Judd

133. Where was Hank Williams buried?

Montgomery, AL

134. What song did Hank Williams Sr. and his son Hank Jr. sing together many years after Hank Sr's death?

There's a Tear in my Beer

135. What two instruments does Merle Haggard play?

Guitar and Fiddle

136. What singer established the foundation 'Let Them Run' to save the wild horses?

Lacy J Dalton

137. Merle Haggard served three years in San Quinton for what crime?

Burglary

138. Who sang 'Some Broken Hearts Never Mend'?

139. Ronnie Milsap's song 'Let's take the Long Way' where?

Around the World

Country Music Trivia

140. Tanya Tucker went to a driving school to do what?

Drive a Race Car

141. Before becoming a famous singer where did Alan Jackson work?

In the mail room at TNN

142. What type of airplane does Alan Jackson own?

A sea plane.

143. Willie Nelson was served with a tax notice for how much money?

32 million dollars

144. Who was told to take an old cold tater and wait?

Jimmy Dickens (In his song)

Country Music Trivia

145. Who did Waylon Jennings give his seat on a plane to and the plane crashed.

The 'Big Bopper'

146. Don Williams made a Cameo appearance in what movie with Bert Reynolds?

Smoky & the Bandit Two

147. Who wrote 'Crazy Arms' for Ray Price?

Chuck Seals (Dan Seals father)

148. What was the title of Johnny Cash's autobiography?

Man in Black

149. Where was Johnny Cash born?

Kingsland, AK

150. What religion did Donnie & Marie Osborne grow up under?

Mormon

151. How did Dottie West die?

In an auto accident on her way to the Grand Ole Opry

152. Where was Roy Clark born?

Meherin, VA

153. What city had a street named after Mickey Gilley?

Ferriday, LA

154. Where did Glenn Campbell buy his first guitar?

Sears & Roebuck

Country Music Trivia

155. In what city does Aaron Tippin have a street named after him?

Greer, SC

156. Willie Nelson played for what president?

Jimmy Carter

157. What actress did Clint Black marry?

Lisa Hartman

158. Which president did Janie Fricke perform for?

Gerald Ford

159. What is Alan Jackson's favorite TV show?

Andy Griffith

160. On what TV show did Patsy Cline get her first

break?

Jimmy Dean

161. Where was Patsy Cline Born?

Winchester, VA

162. When did Patsy Cline die?

March 5, 1963

163. What song is George Morgan best remember for?

Candy Kisses

164. George Morgan's daughter became a popular singer, who is she?

Lorie Morgan

165. When was singer Little Jimmy Dickens born?

1920

166. What was Ray Price's nickname?

Cherokee Cowboy

167. Who is the oldest living member of the Grand Ole Opry?

Little Jimmy Dickens (At this writing he is 93)

168. Who said, "Every man will get cancer if he lives to be old enough. I don't know why I got it -- I ain't old!" He hopes hopes to play as many as a hundred concert dates in 2013. He is 87.

Ray Price

169. What was Aaron Tippin's first hit?

You've got to stand for something

170. Which singer became a commercial pilot at age 20?

Aaron Tippin

171. What's the name of Andy William's theater in Branson, MO

Moon River

172. Andy Williams was a close personal friend of what president.

John F. Kennedy

173. What was Carl & Pearl Butler's first single?

Don't Let Me Cross Over

174. What was Faron Young's nickname?

The singing sheriff

Country Music Trivia

175. Who was Carl Smith's first wife?

June Carter

176. Who did June Carter marry after she was divorced from Carl Smith?

Johnny Cash

177. Who was included in the Carter Family?

Maybelle, June, Helen and Anita

178. What instrument did String Bean play on the Grand Ole Opry and the Hee Haw show?

Banjo

179. What was Ernest Tubb's nickname?

The Texas Troubadour

Country Music Trivia

180. How tall is Brenda Lee?
4' 9"

181. What did Brenda Lee weigh at birth?
4 pounds – 11 ounces

182. What popular singer did Ricky Skaggs marry?
Sharron White

183. The singing group 'The Whites' what was the father's name?
Buck

184. What was Bill Anderson's nickname?
Whispering Bill

185. For the past 10 years Bill Anderson has been

hosting what show?

County's Family Reunion

186. How does Lynn Anderson like to spend her spare time?

Horse ridding

187. What is known as Lynn Anderson's signature song?

I Never Promised You a Rose Garden

188. What did Jerry Lee Lewis, Mickey Gilley and Jimmy Swaggart have in common?

They were cousins

189. What was the name of Buck Owens Band?

The Buckaroos

190. How did Hawkshaw Hawkins die?

In a plane crash with Patsy cline and Cowboy Copas

191. What popular singer was Hawkshaw Hawkins married to?

Jean Shepard

192. What was the name of Bill Monroe's band?

Blue Grass Boys

193. What was the popular song that gave Kitty Wells her start in Country music?

"It Wasn't God Who Made Honky Tonk Angels"

194. What was Tom T. Hall's nickname?

The Story Teller

Country Music Trivia

195. What was the top song that Tom T. Hall wrote?

Harper Valley PTA

196. What are some nicknames of George Jones?

Thumper, No show Jones and The Possum

197. When George Jones got drunk and his wife took his car keys, how did he get to the liquor store?

On his ridding lawnmower

198. What was Tanya Tucker's first big hit?

Delta Dawn

199. What was Bob Wills' band name?

The Texas Playboys

200. How did Johnny Cash start his concerts?

"Hello I'm Johnny Cash" followed by the song 'Folsom Prison Blues'

Made in the USA
Middletown, DE
14 August 2017